VIRGO HOROSCOPE 2023

Your essential guide to love, money, happiness and using moon magic!

Hi guys,

A warm welcome to all my regular readers and a special hello to all new readers. I aim to provide a comprehensive insight into 2023 with spiritual, psychological insight, and down to earth common sense advice.

Every year when I write these books I just cannot believe how fast the year has gone, and that it's once again time to write and publish the series for the next year.

As many of you know, I've been producing these books since 2014, and boy has the world changed since then and 2023 will be a year of unprecedented change in world terms, that's why I've decided to also do an Astrology book of World predictions which include predictions for countries and certain leaders, because I feel that we need to be forwarded and for armed.

It's important to remember that no matter what is happening in the outside world, we all have our lives to live and karma to resolve and we must enjoy our own unique journey. Remember, we are all meant to be here at this very time, to experience what we are experiencing and we should never underestimate our own power and ability to thrive and make a difference.

Yes, we are all at different points along our own personal journey, but what I want to do with these books is encourage you all to understand your own creativity, power and never to underestimate yourself, to feel lost all to lose a sense of purpose. We are all here for a reason and we all have a valuable contribution to make in different ways, and hopefully my annual books have inspired you to understand your purpose and connect with some inspiration.

Fortunately the Saturn Square Uranus that was happening between Saturn in Aquarius and Uranus in Taurus is now done and dusted, which is a good thing because that was creating an enormous amount of tension within all of us, because the energies of Saturn and Uranus are so different. However, what we have coming this year is Pluto moving into Aquarius, and every time Pluto has changed signs there have been dramatic events worldwide that have changed history: it could be the birth of new countries, technological changes, conflict, economic shifts, innovations and the advent of new philosophies or political systems. So we should all be ready to embrace change with an open mind and we should remember not to be overly concerned with things that we are not able to change, because what we all can change is our attitude and it's always better to be optimistic and proactive.

I've often seen in my career as an astrologer that astrology works best for people who make plans, who act on those plans, who motivate themselves and who don't wait around for things to happen. Good things happen when we take chances, when we get up and seize opportunities or even just envisage then, very little happens we stick to comfort zones, resist change and hang onto the past for dear life, irrespective of the planets.

I always believe that it's important to understand our roots, to know where we come from and how our experiences have shaped us and given us wisdom. Our cumulative heritage is always important, but we can't live in the past, things are changing and we have to keep moving along and adapting, and using our wits and innate dynamic energy to thrive.

Love Lisa

VIRGO HOROSCOPE 2023

This is an excellent year for Virgo because your adventurous spirit is ignited. Now not a lot of people think of Virgo as adventurous, but you are insanely curious, flexible and you're eager for excitement and novelty in your life. Virgo know that knowledge is power and therefore you like to expose yourself to new ideas and you find it very exciting exploring understanding, new concepts, meeting new people and being made aware of different ways of thinking as well as philosophy.

This year your desire to lead, particularly to lead with ideas which inspire the spark of enthusiasm in others, especially in your community, is evident. When you're got an idea, you have the bit between your teeth and you have a strong sense of purpose which motivates and inspires you.

This year gathering information and spreading information is a big feature of the year which brings you a lot of satisfaction and is very rewarding at the same time. You are likely to gather a following and receive recognition, and it's more than likely that you will become known to many more people, so your circles are expanding and so are opportunities to obtain even more information and reach more people.

This is a great year with respect to the fact that positive thinking, visualizations and the law of attraction work really powerfully for you. You are in a good frame of mind, you are more confident and optimistic and that's why you are able to generate good karma for yourself and within your relationship.

While Virgo can often be very self-critical and it's well-known that you can get bogged down in details, this year you're much better at seeing the big picture and focusing on what's really important and that helps you in terms of forgiveness, and also in opening windows of opportunity in romance. In terms of personal development and career prospects, because you are not going to let the details of what went before get you down, you're ready for a fresh, shackle free journey where you fully appreciate that anything can happen and you want to be surprised.

Long-distance travel is certainly a feature this year and it may be part of the important journey you are on, because you are on a journey of renewed self-discovery and self-awareness which can help you reboot your marriage, or invite much better more fulfilling and satisfying relationships into your life.

One dream, one goal, one prize, one soul

This year you are on a quest, you are in pursuit of ideas, it's almost like when something has captured your attention, you chase after it as it becomes totally absorbing and you need to discover more. This is certainly a year of action and leadership.

Virgo is often one who enjoys working quietly in the background and you are known for your diligence and perseverance, however this year there is significantly more action in your life. Once you develop a commitment to something, a cause or a concept, you will make sure that your plans are put into motion and in this you can be incredibly determined.

Knight in shining armor

Virgo is a sign who cares about other people, and it's important in your nature to feel useful and to make a difference, and that side of your nature is enhanced this year. However you like to express that on a wider scale and therefore you like to make your mark on social, community or political matters, where you feel you can affect change and win hearts and minds.

Sexual Healing

The first part of the year is excellent for an improvement in the sexual side of your relationships. Virgo is actually quite amorous, for all your reserved, shy and modest exterior, once you get to know a partner well, you can be quite experimental and even adventurous in the bedroom. The first part of the year sees a lot of energy in the sexual arena, so there's a chance for you and your partner to use their sex life to reinvigorate the whole relationship, to improve intimate understanding and affection, and to once again get excited about the potential the relationship has.

Move closer, feel your bodies real close until...

This year better emotional understanding actually starts by experiencing closeness and intimacy, reintroducing touch and showing the care you have for each other through sexual intercourse. Often a downtown in sex life can mean that you each stop thinking the other finds you attractive and this gives rise to insecurities in the relationship, which drive you apart and can lead to communication going downhill.

From the beginning of this year improving your sex life can increase the confidence you and your partner feel, this feeds into self-esteem and this actually leads to both of you expressing yourself more spontaneously emotionally and that can help you guys over relationship hurdles, because there's no longer this feeling of suppression and holding back.

Salt of the Earth

Mercury, your ruler, is retrograde three times this year in Capricorn, Taurus and Virgo, but because it is always retrograde in an earth sign, this means you are personally very grounded, you have a great deal of self-awareness and more understanding of the way you communicate and the impact that has on your partner in relationships.

There's certainly the opportunity for better understanding and more productive conversations in marriage, simply because you are quite rational and you approach conversations in love with a lot more detachment, which means that you and a partner can work on problems without flying off the handle or getting over sensitive.

True colors shining through

Virgo have greater awareness of who you are, what will fulfill you and what you want from relationships, which can help you to have a lot more success in new relationships. You're less likely to waste your time, or jump into things with low potential or where you're going in at a disadvantage because you're too people pleasing or unable to draw a boundary.

Aiming for the stars

This is quite an ambitious year, but not in the sense of material achievement or career advancement, you are more ambitious in terms of expanding your knowledge and increasing the amount of power you have in your community or your professional sphere. You're all about expanding your knowledge, so you want to be seen as someone who is wise, with noble futuristic ideas and who really cares about people beyond your circle.

The reason you are successful this year is that you start your creative and business projects with a lot of enthusiasm and energy, but you can also moderate this with quite a well-rounded realistic and balanced long-term view, and while sometimes planning comes second, once you've bumped your head a few times, the planning does happen and tends to be rather effective even if as an afterthought.

Getting out of the tangle

Often the problem with Virgo is that you do so much planning and pay so much attention to detail that you almost misses an opportunity because you're not first off the blocks, or you become so bogged down in detail that you become negative and bewildered.

However the advantage you have this year is that you jump right in and gets the ball rolling, and then later has a chance to fine tune the details. This means you already have some practical experience before you get back to the drawing board, which is a massive self confidence boost.

You certainly show a greater desire for progress and adventure and if channeled in the right way, it's totally fine for you to take calculated risks.

A changing world backdrop

Often events in your life happen quite quickly and unexpectedly, these can be events in the outside world or within society that impact your perspective. In fact you are likely to see a lot of change in the world around you, and that can spur you on in your actions and convince you that you are on the right track or at the very least that the only way to go, is to embrace change.

One thing you have to be a little bit wary of, is being swept along in a collective energy and losing control of yourself and your aims. So it's very important for you to stay focused on your integrity and what you're trying to achieve, because many times this year there will be occasions that threaten to blow you way off course, before you're even realized how far you're got from your main objectives.

Passion in fashion

In terms of your relationships, you're more sexually driven and your passionate side comes to the fore. In your relationships, you are quite sexy, you like to introduce sex chat or sexual innuendo. You're seductive, charming and you're more willing to sweep a partner of their feet, but sometimes you lose a bit of the Virgo modesty and you go all in, often exaggerating, but let's be honest you are feeling quite good about yourself and that's great.

The great thing about Virgo in relationships this year is your increased levels of desire and zest for living. You're more energetic and you're also more proactive, so while you can sometimes be a flexible character who takes life as it comes, this year you want to embrace life more fully and introduce a much more vibrant energy to daily life. In terms of dating, you enjoy flirting and impressing a partner and key to dating is spontaneity, fun and a little bit of romance, but nothing to slushy or dramatic. It's all about being playful, exploring together and having a life enhancing journey together.

Commitment?

You are not necessarily wanting to get into a committed relationship this year, so dating should be fun and freedom oriented, rather than something that becomes very controlled, scripted and where you guys live in each other's pockets, barely seeing anybody else outside your bubble.

This year you're looking for a partner who is intelligent, filled with energy, someone who also wants to be adventurous and enjoy life. You probably won't hit it off with someone who is conservative, has a lot of baggage and who is nursing a broken heart or on the rebound.

Many Virgo will be looking for someone a lot younger, particularly because you're got this playful side and you might engage in the odd passionate short term affair.

Marriage Spice

In terms of long term relationships, you and your partner must revisit the sexual chemistry that existed between you as that is definitely something you need more of in the relationship. So your mind should be open to new ways of connecting with each other on a sexual level and being a bit more explorative when it comes to intimacy.

Esoteric vibes

For Virgos who are spiritual or religious, this year can represent a renewal of faith when your religion or spiritual side seems so much more relevant and will inform a lot of your choices.

Suddenly your spiritual growth and your awareness of things going on at the universal level is that much more important to you and you pays attention to these matters, especially synchronicity and coincidences. You may seek more inside through a guru or through your priest, or you could do more reading into philosophical subjects to kind of help you join the dots.

In some cases you may be enthusiastic about exploring new spiritual beliefs, you should be careful however not to get too carried away because the spiritual side of life is one of those spheres, which I talked about before, that could lead you down some Dead End Streets or be a total distraction on what's really important.

Lighting up your life

Mars in Gemini from the year start to March, therefore it has a big impact on Virgo, particularly in the realm of career and destiny. This is a time when you really want to make things happen in your life, you've got a lot more drive and motivation and you're certainly more eager to lead which is not something you can always say for Virgo.

Mars is also the planet of action and achievement, this means you become more 'alpha male' and exert more of your positive energies as you become a lot more decisive and more driven. You can also become slightly more hot-headed and aggressive, but often this is exactly what is needed to jumpstart new initiatives to take life forward.

This is an excellent start of the year because you can take your life by the scruff of the neck and ensure that you are doing your utmost to advance your career, grab new career opportunities and to be a positive and motivating force within your family.

Father Figure

Many Virgos are inspired by being a parent, and you are more likely to want to set a good example, and that means - more than ever - you're interested in leading by example, and showing your children how to live their lives through how you live and love in your life.

Looking for the spotlight

Virgo are not often ambitious, you're geared to service and orientated towards detail. You like to do a good job and are quite happy to work in the background, but this year you're a lot more willing to take on public speaking, be more visible and take decisions, and you are very ambitious. You will work extremely hard until what you want to achieve is completely done.

It's more important this year that you have independent projects into which you can apply focus, rather than having to rely on other people. You need to know that you will see results from your actions and that you can use your own ideas, work to your own schedule and show authority and dominion.

This is an excellent year for those Virgo going freelance, onto commission or setting up their own business, because you're highly self-motivated and enjoys working to your own initiative and vision.

There ain't a cloud in the sky

Mars in your solar tenth house is extremely compatible with Jupiter in Taurus, as both are incredibly optimistic, positive, proactive positions that give you a lot of get up and go, and you have so much more impetus for positive change in your life, for tackling fears and for taking a few risks.

Mars in such a prominent house indicates there are times when you bang your head, and don't get it right simply because you are willing to try new things. But you learn fast and get right on with the progress.

Getting into an intimate bubble

In relationships, the summer months (Northern Hemisphere) can be an excellent time to re-discover the spiritual bond you share with your partner and true intimacy. This is an excellent time for getting away together, going on a retreat, to a spa holiday etc. The ideal type of vacation is something where you can go somewhere totally secluded, feel almost immersed in a bubble and be able to switch off all the problems of home and family life, reenter yourselves, refocus your attention on each other to achieve better communication and understanding.

Sex is a gateway to the new you

This is a very important year for sex, and costumes or props can play a very important part in that. You and your partner may want to read erotica together or to each other. You guys may want to share fantasies or you may want to stimulate your sex life through a little bit of role-play

Due to the fact that Virgo does kickoff the year in such an assertive mood, and because generally you're much more positive and proactive as both Jupiter and Uranus are giving you a huge amount of sparkle and reigniting your adventurous spirit, you're also able to take risks with your identity or sexual identity. You can be a lot more self-assured intimately and therefore you're willing to do things that normally wouldn't feel comfortable or suitable for you.

Thus because you're expanding your identity, this can mean that you're more able to enjoy different scenarios, new games or incorporate different ideas in the bedroom, which can be exciting and can create renewal in the sexual arena and beyond.

The courage to confront

Often Virgo, as a Mercury ruled sign, tends to be a conflict avoider, however this year certain issues cannot be avoided and you're far more eager to confront things head on. You're stronger and more courageous and you're less likely to be found by fear.

During the first half of the year you have the power to conquer anxieties and fears which have previously set you back. There's an opportunity for renewed understanding of your own psychological blocks and hurdles, and with that understanding, you're more able to see these in perspective and not to let them hold you back from true fulfilment and honesty in love.

Making peace with your love history

This may also be a crucial year for you settling differences regarding a past relationship. So if you have been involved in a relationship that became contentious, nasty or over which there was a lingering bad feeling or even legal battles, you have the power to resolve these and put them into the grave. So you have the potential for drawing a line in the sand, however often it's very important for you to get legal advice in dealing with these problems, rather than just struggling on as a lay person. You must remember knowledge is power and that includes legal knowledge.

Speaking your mind

This can be a very difficult year if you have a partner who is incredibly controlling and who shuts you down, because it's very important for you to be able to speak your mind and allow your emotions to run freely. You feel a lot more enthusiasm and is a great deal more willing to open up in 2023, but if a partner is not open to that and wants to lead a very controlled, structured existence and feels threatened by your more leadership orientated gung ho approach, there could be some ructions in that relationship and some power struggles.

Any power struggles in 2023 will occur if your partner is not truly supportive of you, and not fully appreciative of you, and that could reveal some fissures in the relationship that will call some weaker relationships into question.

Fools rush in

Due to the fact you're very enthusiastic and impulsive this year and because you have low impulse control, you tend to act more quickly and you don't always have a clear idea of what your strategy is, this means there's a little bit of bumping your head and some dead end streets, but overall your vision is clear and you will definitely make progress in spite of some short-term setbacks you incur.

Rolling your sleeves up

The first few months of the year are a time when important matters will become a more pressing and demand your attention. You cannot ignore these and you need to focus strongly on these matters. This is a time when your positivity is tested, but also rewarded and so you must attend to these difficult matters, be they emotional matters in relationships, sexual matters or matters to do with heath or tax, with a lot of gusto and tenacity, not being afraid or hiding from anything new that you might need to learn or conquer.

Wheels of fortune

If you are looking for work or a new career, you should take action and do everything you can to find the right job. It's no use sitting back and waiting for an opportunity to drop into your lap, you need to explore far and wide and to keep a totally open mind without ruling anything out by prejudging it. It's highly likely you can find a fulfilling new role and this may well be connected with something working in the outdoors, in the community sphere or with people. More generally careers that involve education, guiding people or helping people get access to the law and justice are favored.

Who's the Boss?

One of the problems this year, is you're more likely to come into conflict with authority figures, including your parents or your in-laws. You don't like being told what to do or held back and you can be very impatient, this means you will definitely lock horns with anyone who tries to tell you what to do and how to do it.

You are less inclined to teamwork and cooperation with colleagues, but you're still quite diplomatic with coworkers and conflicts that arise are usually resolved quite quickly. You're lucky this year in that you get a lot of support, most people are happy to see you finding your feet or your wings, and they want to help you fly.

Inner Resolution

Venus goes retrograde in Leo this year in your domain of secrets, your past, your intuition, your need to retreat and your desire for spiritual evolution.

This Venus retrograde period, along with Jupiter in Taurus gives you a great impetus for more philosophical and spiritual understanding and awareness as to what's going on in your life. There is definitely a struggle between the material and the spiritual realm.

I've mentioned before that many issues come to a head this year and while Virgo has a great zest for career advancement and expansion, this doesn't necessarily mean that money is your motivation, there can be many more interesting motivations that you have, including social goals and also inspirational goals in terms of spreading a message.

What's the real bottom line?

The purpose of the Venus retrograde in the middle of the year is to give you pause for thought, so that you can reflect on what you are achieving, how you are achieving it and how this is making you feel. When you're chasing dollars and cents, it's easy to quantify how profitable you are, but when you are pursuing more intangible goals, it takes a lot more reflection to work out how far you are getting and if you are being successful in what you want to do. You should set aside private space for this reflection or meditation as it can be very enlightening and can help you know what move to make next.

Sorry isn't the hardest word

This is a very important year for forgiveness and healing, and you need to make peace with the past. Forgiveness means forgiving others and forgiving yourself, you need to absolve yourself of guilt and the need to continually torment yourself about past mistakes.

This year is quite cathartic, and you need to possibly meditate on, or achieve some kind of spiritual closure in connection events in the more recent past, so that you can be free of any connected toxicity. So it's up to you to focus clearly on the psychological weights which are holding you down and keeping you trapped in in parochial paradigms, and then you must work on releasing those. Showing effort in this regard leads to you experiencing a great deal of weight lifting from your shoulders as you move ahead without all the guilt and constant berating of yourself.

New Beginnings, Personal goals and Charisma

Mercury which is your ruling planet is retrograde three times this year, each time in an earth sign - that's Taurus Virgo and Capricorn. Thus Mercury will be retrograde in your 1st, 9th and 5th solar house.

The Mercury retrograde periods in May, September December and January will affect you in romance and in relationships you can second guess yourself and you may behave more erratically giving your partner pays for thought. During these phases, it's very important to work on better communication within your relationships, you need to be more aware of how you are coming across and the subtle signals you may give a partner.

While communication is one of the most important elements of relationships for Virgo as a rule, this year it is important for you to focus on non-verbal forms of communication, and therefore you need to learn to show your partner how much you care or are attracted to them. If it's a new relationship, through your eye contact, body language and the way you are tactile and affectionate.

I mentioned before that this is an excellent year for intimacy and deeper emotional understanding, so often because there are problems in communication with misunderstandings, feeling misunderstood or perhaps not finding the right words, it's a fantastic opportunity for you to increase the levels of understanding on a deeper emotional level.

Often with Virgo, words can get in the way. You're inclined to verbalize your feelings and you tend to analyze, and sometimes you can be quite productive in that you try and tie everything up into a neat little boxes and you reject the more sentimental, imaginative or intuitive feelings that yourself and your partner may have.

So this year the beauty in relationships is learning to embrace what is perceptive and what gets said between the lines, it's time to develop a better understanding of your partner's moods and where these stem from, and it's time to be more thoughtful and to develop greater awareness of the kind of psychological drivers that impact your relationship.

This is definitely a year where you should not be as concerned with 'he said she said', or with the facts, you need to look at underlying cause and effect, and that means understanding the psychology and emotions a lot better, and that entails paying attention to the more subtle forces at work in your relationship.

The three Mercury retrogrades are wonderful opportunities to explore and discover things about yourself and your partner, and how this plays out and influences your relationship at a deeper level.

Angels and Demons

The solar eclipses in in April and October trigger Pluto which is in Capricorn and Aquarius this year.

This indicates that detoxing is vital, both on a mental and physical level. It's very important to free your mind and free your body of toxins, so that means ridding yourself of toxic relationships and emotionally draining or toxic situations in your life.

Virgo are by nature minimalist, and this is certainly a good year to embrace that by being more organized, streamlining your life and getting rid of activities or associations that tend to create confusion and distraction in your life.

They say 'tidy house tidy mind' and in the case of Virgo, it's very important to have a tidy workspace, because this can make all the difference to your energy levels and productivity.

I know that most Virgo are quite organized, but you do get your Virgos who are more scatty, who allow paperwork to accumulate and who can get in quite a muddle of organized chaos, and I encourage you this year to do a deep purge of useless and unwanted paperwork, clothing, accessories or items in your home and in your workplace or office.

It's definitely a time to get rid of anxious thoughts that spiral out of control. It's very important to work on harnessing your thoughts and thinking productively about problems while not dwelling. What is essential in both your work life and in terms of the inner conversation you have with yourself, is to avoid excess. Sometimes you overanalyze or tend to go over problems or situations looking for clarity, when the key is to let it all go. So the challenge for you is to arrest troubling thoughts and focus on a serene, calm space and let it all go. If you like meditation, which I know a lot of Virgos don't, definitely give it a go, otherwise things like prayer can also be very helpful as is yoga.

Finances

The ruler of your solar second house of finances, Venus is retrograde in Leo, during the summer months (in northern hemisphere).

This indicates that you may be quite indulgent and inclined to spend money on things which bring you pleasure. It is a certainly an excellent time to invest in creative and artistic hobbies, as one of the themes this year is being able to relax, unwind and let go, and spending money on any product or hobby that helps you do so, is money well spent.

You may spend money going on a retreat with friends or getting away from it all to a place where you can avoid phones and all communication, to have a total de-stress and unwind.

During the summer months doing some not-for-profit work, pro bono work or devoting your time to a charitable cause can bring you a lot of satisfaction. Sometimes doing good deeds, giving back or donating money makes you feel a lot better than simply spending on the material.

Sometimes during the summer months, it's not all about satisfaction from spending and earning, there is a lot of pleasure and an internal sense of peace, that can actually be achieved by donating time or money, or pursuing activities that do not have any financial outcome or reward.

Communication, short distance travel and innovation

The ruler of your third solar house of communication Pluto is squared by Jupiter in the spring months of the northern hemisphere, and this is an excellent time for taking a short break, for spontaneous journeys or road trips.

This is an ideal time to respond to whims, to be spontaneous and to satisfy your curiosity. During this period you should be open to sudden changes and doing things a little bit differently.

This is an excellent time to work with new colleagues, to go on trips with colleagues or to study as part of your job. It can be very rewarding hanging out or being with new colleagues, and in some cases you may develop a strong friendship with a new colleague or even romance.

This is an excellent time for journalistic work or research and it's also a wonderful time for collating and editing a vast volume of information that you need to categorize, condense or summarize as that can be something you can easily do, it's rewarding too.

This is a highly productive time, so any work that you need to do in connection with IT, sales, admin or logistics can be tackled during the spring months with great efficiency and progress.

Home and Family

The middle part of the year may be a time when you consider a home move, this is a very good time for real estate and property deals. The summer months in the Northern Hemisphere are also a good time to undertake a renovation or restoration project.

You may be inclined to do home renovations or extensions, and if you buy a new home this is an also an ideal time to do up a property that is severely run down.

In terms of family relationships, it's important to have boundaries and know when to say NO. Things can become quite emotionally charged on the family front, so you need to know when to walk away. Some family members can be more in need of emotional support and while you are happy to give it, it can be quite draining and you have to know when to back off.

While some family members, both older and younger, may need your help, it's important for you not to try and live their lives for them. So know when you have given enough advice and it's time to let them take responsibility, you don't want to be immersing yourself in their lives or problems, there is a degree to which they have to take ownership and agency of their own lives.

Marriage

Neptune continues to be in the third decan of Pisces which is in your solar 7th house of marriage. It's important for you to develop compassion and understanding, remember to work on the emotional closeness you have with your partner.

It's vital to take a philosophical approach to marriages and relationships, it's important to go with the flow and not try and micromanage or control everything that happens. There is a lot going on within your partner's life that you can't necessarily control and that's why you need to let it be.

It's in the nature of Virgo to strive to understand and make sense of things in your life, but you have to learn to do that from a spiritual perspective. Often what happens now in marriage has a higher purpose or meaning that is quite difficult to understand and may only be understood in hindsight, so it's important for you not to be self-critical or to beat yourself up, remember to be kind to both yourself and your partner and to use your spiritual will to navigate relationship issues.

This can potentially be a year of great romance, so don't forget to indulge with your partner in things that you both find magical, whether it's movies, music, poetry etc. It's time to make a space in your life for fantasy and escapism together i.e. little romantic getaways to somewhere secluded where the world cannot intrude.

21

JANUARY

Essence and Energies – "Shout to the top"

This is the month to take things to the next level, so the challenge for you is to push yourself to attain that next step. Now this may be being more ambitious and going for a promotion, it could be being a little bit more daring and challenging yourself to aim higher in a certain sport or creative hobby, or it can be looking for a new level of depth in relationships.

Your biggest enemy right now is being passive and resting on laurels, so you need to capitalize on whatever situation you are in and expect more. Sometimes Virgos settle for second best, sometimes because you are modest and can be people pleasing, but right now it's quite ok to expect more from yourself and others and for you to push through to the next level.

Affirmation: "I chose to move beyond my fears and limits with courage and enthusiasm for success."

Love and Romance

This is a very important month for establishing new relationships and you could easily find yourself magnetically drawn to someone, and yet this person may be elusive and unavailable, so the relationship could start with a lot of complications. However you shouldn't be deterred from pursuing new relationships just because on paper they look a difficult, confusing or there a lot of obstacles. It is certainly true right now that the path of true love is never smooth so you should anticipate a long, winding road but you should be ready to grab that with excitement not trepidation.

A new person that comes into your life can be both annoying and exciting, they trigger you in good ways and bad ways, but they are also a spur that allows you to understand more about yourself, and they may just be a catalyst to help you embrace new ways of thinking that set you on the exciting path of adventure that is 2023.

This is an important month of the year for Virgos who are involved in romances, this is a month of crisis and turning points in love, it's a time when a partner will either prove himself to you in a good way or a bad way, but either way you should get some clarity, even if you don't find out everything that you necessarily want to.

It's important to be alert to signs and signals in love, you don't want to be like an ostrich, if there is something that is causing you concern, you really want to investigate it seriously. So this is a time when you may need to have some slightly more difficult and possibly emotive conversations with a partner, just to find out if you're on the same page and if you both agree on where the relationship is going.

Career and Aspiration

With Mars direct in Gemini this month, there's a huge amount of energy available for you to pursue new career options, to open doors for yourself and to find a new job. This is an excellent time for Virgo who are unemployed or unhappy in your current job to make that break and start a concerted effort to find something new that is much more rewarding.

This is an excellent month for research, investigation and showing determination and courage in pursuing a goal. If you are very dedicated to the job you do and have a great deal of desire to excel, you can become quite obsessive and fixated this month, but you should see some stunning results. You tend to work very hard and nothing deters you and if there's something that you believe needs to be done, you will do it despite criticism or doubt from others, and you will be proved to have had the right approach.

This is a time to leave no stone unturned when pursuing career goals, you should not neglect to follow up a lead, an opportunity or a bit of information.

Adventure and Motivation

This month there is a great deal of fun to be had in pursuing your hobbies, particularly your more eccentric hobbies. If you have any interests which involve a lot of attention to detail, research or mechanical assembly this is an excellent month.

Virgo is particularly attracted to things like chess, puzzles or games that require a certain amount of skill in assembling something. So if you enjoy crafts, sculpture or carpentry, this can be an activity which is immensely rewarding as you find it quite satisfying to take out your frustrations or escape from the world while fine tuning stuff, using microscope to glue intricate little pieces together or fixing something.

January is ideal for joining a gym and starting a long-term health and fitness plan, however you should start as you mean to go on, you should avoid anything faddish. Choose a diet and exercise plan that you know suits your personality and your lifestyle and that you are therefore more likely to stick with.

This is not a good time to sign up for any health routine that you feel is going to be boring, very strenuous or unpleasant. You should make sure there is an element of anticipation and excitement about starting a new fitness or diet, because this will ensure its success.

Marriage and Family

With Mars and Venus affecting your sphere of marriage, what's important this month is communication and renewed understanding. So whatever happened last year, it's time for you and your partner to reopen the channels of communication and to begin getting used to sharing with each other. Often last year things got in the way of effective communication, but at the beginning of this year it's time to show each other you care by being understanding and by sharing a genuine interest in what the other is going through.

So the question you should both be asking each other this month, is, "How are you? No really, how are you?" You guys don't want to be asking rhetorical questions that don't bring about meaningful replies, it's very important for you to set aside time to have conversations that are productive, and that you both work walk away from feeling emotionally satisfied and feeling that you've been understood, at least partially, or that cooperation is returning to the relationship.

Money and Finance

This can be a very good month for you refinancing, you may be able to reorganize your finances so that you can pay down debt or consolidate.

It's definitely worth understanding the tax code better so you can arrange your financial affairs to take advantage of tax savings. It may also be important for you to understand changes to laws and regulations because you may be entitled to claim certain benefits.

It's likely that money can come to you in unexpected ways, you may receive a gift, a legacy, some donations or generosity from clients.

If you works in financial management you may receive a substantial new contract or big client.

Living and Loving to the Full

This month is an important month to solidify commitment in love, so activities like renewing your vows or talking about how important the relationship is to you both and affirming the bond is vital.

Showing strong levels of commitment is very important, so the way to enhance love magic is to show each other appreciation, gratitude and do small acts of kindness that mean a lot. It's important to be thoughtful as the little things really do add up.

So this month is not so much about grand romantic gestures or anything particularly flamboyant, showy or glitzy, it's more about random acts of kindness that show you care for each other.

Planetary Cautions

Mercury retrograde is in Capricorn until the 19th meaning that although you're very likely to meet someone new during this phase as you're very curious in love and eager to get into the dating game, it can actually be quite tricky.

You are undecided in love, which is why long distance relationships that develop now work well as there is that distance, that perspective from which you can assess the potential of the relationship without getting to close and intimate too quickly.

You need to go with your head in love during this period, to set emotion and sentimentality aside and to be objective. If you are rather maudlin or heart on sleeve, then be cautious as you're not necessarily going to make good decisions in this frame of mind.

You can suddenly get cold feet in new relationships and so relationships can be stop start. In relationships in general, you may suddenly need a bit more space or you could create an injection of excitement with new social activities.

Moon Magic

The new moon phase extends from the 21th of January to the 5th of February, this waxing phase is the perfect fortnight for new initiatives, setting plans, establishing goals, starting anything prospective and being proactive. This is the action phase, details below:

Mercury goes direct on 19th indicating that the communications sphere, short journeys, job interviews, public speaking, teaching and multi-tasking are once again very successful. This period marks an excellent phase for personal creativity and new ways of presenting yourself.

Sun Sextile Jupiter at the new moon favors psychological renewal, affirmations, creative visualization and gaining insight. This is a great time for artistic work. It's also a good time for retreats and meditation. Venus Conjunct Saturn indicates a good time for new romance, dating and social activities. A great waxing period for leisure activities or business connected to entertainment.

Financial matters and investment in assets are not favored. This is not a good time for international travel or new international business contracts. Publishing and advertising are not favored.

Essence and Energies – In the hunt

This month you need to focus on the satisfaction of a job well done. In order to dominate your chosen profession or be more competitive, you need to be able to stay the pace of the race, but that doesn't mean that you have to go out in front or always lead, it means staying with the pack then seizing your opportunity when the time arises.

It's important for you to be patient and wise in your sense of timing, as it's very confidence boosting if you can strive towards a goal, withstand the challenges, stay focused and in control and then use a strong sense of willpower and your own knowledge to grab the prize.

This month it's all about knowing the ideal time to seize a victory and then not being afraid to go for it.

So work hard, but be ambitious.

Affirmation: "I have the courage and confidence to weather the storms, stay in the hunt and reach my personal pinnacle."

Love and Romance

This month Virgo is indecisive when it comes to love and you may find yourself on the horns of a dilemma. The theme in love this month is indecision and a battle between head and heart.

You are likely to be involved in a romantic relationship that is all-consuming and could be quite unsettling as in one way your head may be thinking of all the negatives, but your heart feels inexplicably drawn to this person. This can cause a lot of conflict internally, and that conflict or these ambivalent feelings can be telegraphed to a new partner who may wonder what you really feel.

You need to be honest with yourself, and acknowledge that the new relationship you're in is not what you're normally used to, and you don't feel safe, but you should keep moving forward and engage your adventurous spirit. If you are not able to think through the internal conflict, it will be picked up by your partner who may become very insecure and little bit possessive, simply because they sense your indecision.

Career and Aspiration

This month work can be tiring and not very fulfilling, and therefore you need to look after your health. It's very important for you to have strong boundaries and when you walk out of the office, you need to say 'enough is enough' and you need to turn off the phone and shut down the email. It's very easy for your work to encroach on the rest of your life, so you have to ensure that you have a work-life balance that enables you time to decompress and de-stress.

So the message in work this month, is be diligent, be controlled, follow through and be systematic. Often this month things can feel like an uphill battle, but if everything is tackled in a methodical way you will eventually get through it.

This is not a good month to hire new staff or outsource as the quality of work could be questionable and it may not work out as planned.

This is also not a good month to work with animals in terms of looking after them, training them or services for them.

Adventure and Motivation

This month there could be some excitement in the work arena, particularly relating to new colleagues from another country who are being trained by you or who are bringing new ideas to your work space. Often an international and exotic element enters the frame in terms of your work life, and this adds a whole new perspective that can make work seem a lot more fun and exciting.

There may even be the opportunity for international travel via your work, and even if you don't travel as such you should have more contact with different cultures, people with different perspectives etc. This can make work a lot more interesting, it can also suddenly spark a sense of what is possible within you, and an important bit of information could fall into your lap which you can use to start your own business.

This is a time when you want to impress on others that you will not be taken for granted, that you know your rights and you understand when you are being walked all over.

There is a sense this month that you need to prevail, you need to have faith in yourself, you need to understand who you fundamentally are, and you need to have a clear sense of being deserving and worthy, and this will help you to be more ambitious in all walks of life and more able to assert your rights.

It is also a time to be more in tune with your aggressive impulses. Virgo tend not to be people who understand the value of sometimes being a little bit pushy and domineering, but it is certainly time this month to get in touch with your fire cracker energy.

Marriage and Family

During this month there's a lot of potential for romance and having some tender, quiet moments with your partner. If you are both in the mood, you guys can stimulate affection once more and can use your relationship as an escape and a refuge from all the worries of the world. It may be ideal for you to have a little escape, or if you can't afford an escape, have a quiet candlelit dinner in your home, send the children to the grandparents and turn all the devices off.

It's highly likely that you and your partner are facing a lot of ambivalence about your relationship, or about the immediate future, and this can create quite a lot of anxiety. Therefore it's very important for Virgo and your partner to find a quiet and safe space where you will both be understood and you can honestly discuss your fears and anxieties, about family life, your relationship or about your guys' future. I'm not saying that this is a time where you will reach conclusions, but you definitely need to be honest and put your cards on the table, because the motto this month is, "a problem shared is a problem halved".

The key is learning to enjoy your partner's company again in a relaxed environment, and letting that lead the way to renewing a physical and emotional bond. The key however, is no pressure, you don't want to be forcing each other into situations where a lot of insincerity or pretense is involved. It's a case of circulating love back into the relationship by making the ambiance conducive through harmonious, pleasant, relaxed time spent together.

Money and Finance

The key this month is using tried and tested methods, you should continue to work with the people who have proved reliable in the past and you should nurture those contacts. It's very easy for you to be lured into new associations that promise much or seem to offer some sort of financial Nirvana, but all that glitters is not gold this month! Good strategies, hard work and renewing bonds with trusted reputable people pay off in terms of money, but getting carried away by people who offer very exciting but speculative prospects are not a good way forward.

Living and Loving to the Full

The keyword in enhancing love relationships is 'compassion'. It's important that you both show each other understanding and empathy. So often in day to day life it's easy to focus on the pragmatic or immediate issues of concern and often emotional matters are pushed to the bottom of the pile.

Virgo tend to be very pragmatic, yes you are sensitive and you are thoughtful and often you expresses this in pragmatic ways by being helpful, but this month it is important for you to show your support for your partner emotionally, and that can mean being a good listener, being there and using touch and warmth as a way of showing support. So often it's not necessarily advise your partner is after, it's just knowing that you understands, you get it and the way you can show that is often through being close physically and offering hugs, because hugs are healing and sometimes words just get in the way.

Planetary Cautions

This can be a tricky month to work with other people, you should avoid working with people who are disorganized, lazy or who don't pull their weight, because this could be extremely frustrating for you. So if you have a choice, you need to pick the people you works with wisely and if there are colleagues who show a disrespectful or careless attitude to their work, you need to keep far away from them and not allow yourself to be tarnished by then attitude to service.

Work with clients and customers can be very demanding and very trying as they tend to soak up a lot of your time. So it's very important for you not to take on any new clients and customers, because existing ones may be a handful enough.

Moon Magic

The new moon phase extends from the 20th of February to the 7th of March, this waxing phase is the perfect fortnight for new initiatives, setting plans, establishing goals, starting anything prospective and being proactive. This is the action phase, details below:

The waxing phase is excellent for new fitness routines and weight loss or dietary goals. A good time to join a gym. This is a great time for streamlining and getting more organized to make the year more efficient. Delegating and outsourcing can be good avenues of activity. A good period to recruit.

Sexual understanding and better intimate communication in relationships is likely. An excellent time to improve sex life.

Debt and financial matters may see improvement. There can be luck in receiving gifts, donations, tips and unexpected income. A good time for discussion about money matters and savings goals in your marriage.

Better psychological awareness and content leads to resolution of anxiety and fear.

Essence and Energies – "Is this the real life, is this just fantasy?"

This month is all about using your emotional intelligence, it's about being more perceptive about other people and understanding who they really are, what inspires and what motivates them. Virgo are by nature quite critical, you are very canny, and you are analytical thus you are usually very good at spotting other people's weaknesses and that trait can be particularly helpful this month.

It's vital not to take people at face value, it is important for you to appraise them, assess them and figure out both from a logical and intuitive standpoint where they are coming from.

Remember to be a little bit detached both in relationships and when meeting strangers, don't allow people to play on your emotions, stay vigilant, remain objective and don't get distracted when other people try and divert you with lies, illusions, drama or deceptive behavior.

Affirmation: "I rise above the emotions and angst of the moment and I see the bigger picture."

Love and Romance

Virgo may find that a new partner wants to solidify a relationship very quickly and become very serious. Now the problem here is Virgo prefers to take it rather slowly in relationships in terms of the commitments side, yes you want to enjoy a passionate and meaningful relationship with a new person, and you want to be loyal, but you definitely don't want to commit this year. So being faced with a partner who is putting a lot of pressure on you for definitive answers about the future can be a tricky prospect. You need to strike a balance between reassuring a new partner and letting them know that your feelings are genuine, while also saying to them that you have a lot on your plate and you don't feel in a position to provide guarantees about your own future, never mind a future with someone. So a partner will have to be patient, but you may have to have a difficult discussion to convey this to a partner.

This is possibly not one of the best months of the year to get into a new relationship, particularly a long distance relationship, you simply will not have enough information about a person, and they might be not be forthcoming, they could be outright deceptive or they could be guilty of errors of omission in a new relationship. So while it's highly likely that you could become quite captivated and almost infatuated with someone right now, you need to take those rose colored glasses off and see things for what they are, otherwise you could end up becoming disappointed or hurt.

Career and Aspiration

In terms of your career, you don't get the necessary support you want from other people in March, so it's important for you to trust yourself, to trust your judgement to do your own research and to be an independent thinker.

This month success is often a lonely journey, there may be people who are jealous of your success or threatened by it, and therefore won't support you, or you may be in a new field where the people you used to know are not able to help you, so you have to use your own instincts and you must rely on your innate Virgo versatility.

It's also very important right now for you to be adaptable and observant, things are changing very quickly and therefore you need to have lots of different strategies that you can jump between. Being stubborn will not work right now, and so when something proves not to be heading in the right direction you mustn't be afraid to quickly change tack.

Adventure and Motivation

This is a very good month for working with people and collaborating, particularly on projects of an artistic or performance nature. However, when it comes to matters that pertain to legal, financial or practical matters, then you need to choose who you work with very, very carefully.

In matters of entertainment, if things go wrong it's not life and death, therefore you can choose to be more liberal and open minded about the sort of people you unite to work with or develop symbiotic relationships with. However, this is a more difficult time for working with people as things can go wrong if there is deception or if people are simply not up to it. You'll have to really be careful about testing people to see if they have competency, because someone may, on the surface, look like they know what they're doing, but when it comes to it they might not.

Marriage and Family

This month it's important for you to be straightforward, it's very easy for misunderstandings and communication to make relationships extremely complicated and a little bit upsetting, and that means a lot of care must be taken to communicate in a concise way that doesn't leave anything open to interpretation.

It's probably not the best month for any surprises, jokes, using a lot of innuendo etc. because these things can be open to interpretation, they may offend or they may further complicate an already murky and foggy environment in relationship. Your partner may be feeling particularly vulnerable right now, so it's not a good time for you to be off hand, to be critical or to be flirting with other people, so all those are a no no! You must be more cognizant of your partner's feelings and not pushing her buttons.

Money and Finance

This can be a good month for money, but at the same time they can be some dramatic changes in terms of your priorities or the way in which you make your money.

A change in career, or a change to your financial position could lead to an adjustment phase, but overall all there's a certain amount of luck this month and things are going your way and this can help see you through.

In terms of money, fortune favors the brave and you may have to take a certain amount of risk this month simply because there are a lot of unknowns. However you also have the potential to make money if you act quickly, so your Virgo analytical skills, along with the ability to think quickly can certainly help you to capitalize where others can't.

Living and Loving to the Full

For Virgo, truth and self-respect are very important ingredients for you in life, but particularly in relationships. However you're also a conflict avoider and a people pleaser, so on occasion you can lose touch with the importance of truth in a relationship, and when that isn't fully there, it can damage the relationship without you even realizing that that is the cause. So in order to enhance your love magic this month, you must introduce truth and honesty back into the relationship and that means that you may have to have candid and difficult discussions. You also may have to redraw boundaries: it's very important for you, once again, to establish in your relationships where enough is enough, and where they should be a separation between your partner and your own emotions.

It's time for you to face up to certain facts about your relationships and start looking for solutions rather than acting as if these problems don't exist.

Planetary Cautions

This month it's important for you to avoid misinformation, timewasters and detractors. You may be running into people who either don't have your best interests in mind or who are looking to potentially cause trouble or sow seeds of doubt in your mind.

You need to quickly assess whether people are doing activities or have information that is worth its salt, and if not you should avoid those people. You must understand that you are judged by the company you keeps and you must avoid people who have a lack of integrity or dubious intentions.

Essence and Energies – "Gonna get Dressed for Success"

The essence this month is building strong foundations, it's important for you to focus on things which increase your inner strength.

Doing activities which require a lot of self-control can help increase your sense of self-esteem, and this can make you more secure. So sometimes sticking to a very strict diet or doing a rigorous exercise or yoga routine at the same time and place every day can help give you that feeling of control.

Virgos often like routines and rituals, in some ways you can be a little bit superstitious, and right now these routines and rituals can add a great deal of stability to your life, they can bring order to your thinking and they can help you to establish more security, which in turn helps you to build a strong emotional foundation.

So the mission right now is about developing good routines, positive mindsets and getting into good habits that you can take forward to reinforce self-improvement and create solid foundations in your life.

Affirmation: "I resolve to develop position and progressive new habits and rituals which reinforce my inner strength."

Love and Romance

Love and romance in April can produce quite strong and intense feelings, however it is also a time that's quite confusing because of the mercury retrograde.

Mars in Cancer indicates that platonic relationships can suddenly become something that is more enticing sexually and you can experience a high level of attraction or desire towards someone in your friendship circle. So while new sexual friendships can begin, a sexual relationship can begin with someone who you have known a long time.

This can also be a rather turbulent relationship as it's likely to trigger things within you, it may be that a new partner causes you to second-guess yourself, but this could also encourage positive changes in your life, simply because this person holds up a mirror to you and maybe cajoles or encourages you towards positive change internally.

Your strength in love right now is your adaptability and your compassion, but your weakness is that you are not clear enough on what you want and you fail to assert your needs and when you kinda 'wake up' it may be too late. You have to be very careful right now not to lose the initiative, as it is very easy to just sink passively into something where you underestimate how far in you are and that there may be not turning back. The key now is awareness, and so you need caffeine emotionally or else you can sleepwalk into a problem. Think self-protection in relationships and don't be too heart on sleeve.

Career and Aspiration

This is an excellent month for team and group orientated activities, you definitely need to use your diplomatic and social skills to encourage other people to work together and to increase the morale of the workforce or your staff.

This is a good time for you to inject energy into your networks and to encourage people to come together in terms of seminars, conferences or going to trade fairs. You must encourage the sharing of information and more proactive responses to changes within your industry or the economy in general.

So you should be looking for any opportunity to collaborate with others, to share information with others, to work with others and to inspire other people within your industry.

This month it's all about using your soft skills and people power, you must be charming, charismatic and show social leadership by encouraging cooperation between different groups of people.

Adventure and Motivation

Virgo tend to be very self-aware and you take delight in knowing yourself well, so a lot of the enjoyment this month comes from experiencing life on an esoteric or mysterious level. You need to get in touch with your true nature and you can get benefit from achieving psychological understanding, so there is a strong desire to delve into the mysteries of your own personality or your psychology and uncover what lies beneath your more obvious traits.

There is a possibility now for a significant transformation psychologically, you have the ability to conquer fears, anxieties and bad habits, and therefore a lot of the satisfaction you get out of this month is by being able to close chapters, to get the albatross off your neck and free yourself from anything psychological that is bogging you down.

Marriage and Family

In terms of marriage, this can be the beginning of a major new phase of development between yourself and your partner. In fact what is about to change in your relationship could lead to the relationship becoming that much more valuable, and loyalty and commitment will thus increase.

However compromise is necessary, you and your partner may have to rein in some activities or close something down in order to re-focus on the relationship and tap into all the wonderful benefits that there are. This is not a time to procrastinate or run on tangents, it's time for a concerted effort to put the past behind you and embrace new opportunities and possibilities together with a positive and proactive mindset.

This is an excellent time to settle differences, but it's also an important time for you and your partner to settle differences from past relationships that may still be casting a shadow into the current relationship.

In existing relationships competitiveness can be a problem as it grates, but in new relationships it is quite stimulating and even sexy. You will be the driving force in your new relationships where you initiate events, activities and sexual advances and you will demand a strong reciprocity, however timing is a problem as your partner may not share your high sex drive or they may be suffering from fatigue which means they are not feeling at their best.

Money and Finance

This can be an excellent period for you in terms of money, you may be fortunate in getting a loan, loan extension or a reduced interest rate. It's well worth you shopping around and having discussions with your bank ager because you may just be able to get a preferential deal.

This is also a time when you could benefit from passive income i.e. receiving donations and an increase in subscriptions or royalties, so sometimes money comes to you as a result of work done in the past, rather than this month or through salary.

It may be that your partner getting a new job or job promotion helps the family finances in general, alternatively a relative could show some generosity in lending or giving you some money.

Living and Loving to the Full

This month the way for Virgo to enhance love, is to be totally honest with yourself, and to let go of any unhealthy habits or attachments in your life that are actually hindering understanding or better love making.

One thing that you should pay attention to is an obsession with social media or things like Twitter, because these could be eating into intimate time and intruding on your emotional life. Social media is often a very destructive force because it takes attention away from your partner, your partner's needs, your partner's emotions etc., and so that not only verbal communication breakdown breaks down, but you're less likely to pick up psychically and intuitively the subtle signals that your partner is giving, because you're so focused on either social media or work, or because of the ever presence of a mobile phone.

So no distractions in the bedroom.

Planetary Cautions

With Mercury going retrograde in Taurus, this may not be the best month for long haul journeys and significant business travel.

This also isn't a good time to begin a course of higher education or change something significant about your education goals, even though you may not be satisfied, you should stick with what you're doing for a while and see if it ends up working itself out.

This isn't a good time to start my divorce proceedings or get involved in any legal battles with people or government, mediation should be pursued as far as possible.

Publishing, seeking publicity and promotional activities in general are not favored.

We all have places where we stuff things away to be dealt with another day, this applies to home or office, there are places where you hide away old paperwork or put things out of sight out of mind.

The focus this month is dealing with all those things that are usually are out of sight out of mind, with a positive attitude, to get rid of these things or deal with the various problems they represent.

Secondly, it's especially important to deal with any sentimental items or old correspondence with which there are emotional attachments. It is quite important for you in April to purge certain thoughts and people from your mind, and often getting rid of physical things connected to certain events or people is a sign to the university that you want to move on, and it can help you reinforce psychological purging.

Moon Magic

The new moon phase extends from the 20th of April to the 5th of May this waxing phase is the perfect fortnight for new initiatives, setting plans, establishing goals, starting anything prospective and being proactive. This is the action phase, details below:

The waxing phase is excellent for mass communications, social media marketing and journalism. Research and investigation is successful.

Internally this is an excellent time for self-awareness and meditation.

Group goals and networking or social media marketing is supercharged. Market research is important.

Mercury retrograde in Taurus on 21st means that a certain amount of caution is needed in terms of public speaking and so research must be solid as you are under the microscope. The Mercury retrograde period does not favor job interviews, job applications, new career moves and dealing with authority. Short distance travel and IT projects are not favored.

Essence and Energies – "Stay on these roads"

This month the essence is expansion, awareness of opportunity and doing brand new things so that you can gain experience and insight into different aspects of life. It is very important to have an open mind and you have to be happy to take a few risks, and when I say risks I don't mean acrobatics, skydiving or gambling on the stock market, I simply mean getting out of comfort zones and challenging yourself by setting the bar quite high.

This is a month where they can be some surprises, some shocks and all your preconceptions are challenged, so if you embrace the month with the idea of learning, having a little bit of an adventure and enjoying a dynamic atmosphere, you will be all the better for it. So you don't want to go into this month with a rigid, boring mindset, seek new ways of seeing the world, and look for circumstances that don't fit in with your old paradigms.

Affirmation: "I face every new opportunity without flinching and I resolve to embrace and enjoy change."

Love and Romance

This month, the ruler of your house of romance is entering into Aquarius, and while it will be in Aquarius for two decades its entry into Aquarius is still something quite significant.

This indicates that you're entering a whole new phase in terms of love, romance and dating. Old paradigms and expectations go out the window and you are ready to totally embrace what is bohemian and a little bit exotic in terms of your love life.

During this time you can develop a very strong relationship with someone whom you work with, a fellow professional or someone who shares interests of yours. Intellectual curiosity and friendship are vital to love relationships forming, however they will be a big element of passion and desire, and so new relationships will revolve around mutual interests and a great sex life.

Venus in Cancer is trining Saturn which is in Pisces which means that this is a good time for both new and old relationships. Emotions tend to be more stable, relationships fall into a happy pattern and it's a time when you could become closer and even difficult relationships should feel more harmonious right now. This is quite a productive phase in love when you can work together as there is a high level of cooperation and camaraderie.

It's very important to work on the friendship factor in love, it's important to be each other's companions, you should not be critical of each other, you should be supportive as it's very important to share in each other's interests and to be mutually encouraging.

Career and Aspiration

This month sudden changes within political and the economic world will impact your business decisions, but this should be in a positive way in terms of creating more opportunities so you must keep an open and positive attitude.

You should expect the unexpected, there will be surprises and shocks this is a month, where even things that seem 100-percent certain are not unfolding so, and this you cannot have rigid views or expectations.

Going ahead in your career, you can no longer see the world through the same lens, new circumstances do not fit in with your old views and so any viewpoints or ideas that you had previously associated yourself with may now have to be adjusted, so that you can gain more understanding and insight of what appropriate new approaches are.

Out with the old, in with the new and expect to be surprised is the key.

Adventure and Motivation

This can be a time when you quickly gather a following and people begin to react favorably to your ideas. So while the first part of the month, in the

Mercury retrograde period, isn't great for publishing, teaching or putting forward your ideas, after the retrograde period is an excellent time for those activities. Blogging, vlogging or getting involved in social and political discussions can gain you a great deal of acknowledgement from others, accolades and also success

During this time you may be more successful in competition, at both sporting and intellectual competition, and you should share that success with others as a great deal of satisfaction can be gained through mentoring, coaching others or indeed throwing parties to reward everyone that was part of your success.

This may not be a good month for international travel simply because of the huge amount of uncertainty regarding travel and sudden economic and social events.

This is an excellent time for enhancing your life through self-development, so if there are any courses, seminars or training that you want to undertake which you feel will help you to find your aptitude or tap into your potential and become more confident, this is an excellent time to do that.

This is an ideal time to embrace an alternate path, so if you are interested in any alternative practices from alternative healing, alternative political viewpoints etc. this is the time to no follow those with energy.

Marriage and Family

Sometimes marriage is last on the list simply because you are very busy with a focus outside of the marriage, so loyal and stable marriages tend to thrive right now if your partner and you have a really good understanding on each other's needs and aspirations, and if your partner is loving and supportive. This month should flow smoothly, there should be harmony in the relationship and your partner will be very supportive of you and happy to cheer you on, as long as there is generally good communication.

If your partner is not supportive of your ideas or doesn't quite appreciate where you are at this year in terms of wanting to explore and be more adventurous, then this is a time where some difficult conversations need to be had, and there may be a slight period of cooling off or distance occurs.

Your partner may take a step back as they begin to adjust to some of the things that you are now pursuing or aiming for in your life.

In general you have a very positive energy this month and your partnership benefits from that, but sometimes your partner - if they are not in a very happy frame of mind - may be slightly threatened by your independence and adventure.

Money and Finance

This is generally a positive month for finances, you seems to be able to find new business opportunities and ways of bringing money in.

New opportunities can arise within your networks or there can be new opportunities related to information, so a piece of news or change in the political climate can all trigger a chain reaction that you can capitalize on.

You generally benefit this month financially where you work closely with others in your professional community to share information and exchange ideas or find creative solutions together.

Changes in terms of computer technology can also be very important to explore, and you need to be abreast of the latest technological changes affecting your industry.

Living and Loving to the Full

This month the key to enhancing love relationships and your attitudes in general is positive affirmations and gratitude.

Central to the theme this month is a renewed hope, faith and an understanding of how blessed you is, so it's important for you to give thanks, see the glass as half-full and take it from there.

It's time to look at relationships with fresh eyes and to allow inspiration to come into your life by being open to possibilities and not rejecting anything, or continuing with very closed mindsets.

You must examine all your beliefs connected with limitation, you must analyze the warning lights in your head and the times when you say 'no, I can't' and see if they should rather be amber lights or times to say 'yes, I can '.

You are entering a more loving phase in your life, you will be filled with vibrant energy, mental clarity and a deeper understanding of yourself and others around you which will enhance all love relationships.

Planetary Cautions

Until Mercury goes direct on the 15th of the month you should continue to be cautious in international trade and in dealing with the legal system.

Activities involving publicity and promotions are still not advised and you should be very cautious of throwing money in this direction.

This is not a good time to have the in-laws over to stay and it's important for you and your partner to resist any advice or interference from your respective parents.

This is a good time for further study, clarification and understanding legal fine print.

It's very important now for you to not take risks, to look before you leaps and not to exaggerate anything because at the moment it's easy to be overly optimistic, so some caution is advisable.

Moon Magic

The new moon phase extends from the 19th of May to the 3rd of June this waxing phase is the perfect fortnight for new initiatives, setting plans, establishing goals, starting anything prospective and being proactive. This is the action phase, details below:

This is not the best month for totally new activities especially ones that need a lot of confidence and physical energy.

This is not the most favorable month for a major career change, job interviews or putting proposals towards the boss.

This is a good month for recruitment and outsourcing, for improving technology and efficiency in the workplace. This is another good month for health and fitness goals, starting new diets and using holistic methods to improve health.

Home improvements and property matters are not favored this month, this is not a good time to house hunt, move home or renovate your home to an extensive degree.

This is an excellent time for romance, brand new relationships, dating and social occasions. A good time for planning entertainment and leisure activities for personal enjoyment or business, and an ideal time to work with children.

Essence and Energies - "That's me in the spotlight"

This month the essence is flexibility, fun and curiosity. One of the strengths of Virgo is your ability to adapt quickly to changing circumstances, another one of your abilities is communication skill and knowing how to strike the right notes with people. So I want to encourage you this month to be ready to debate an engage with others, to go to meetings, to have discussions and show that you are willing to not only engage with people but to incorporate their ideas.

This month you should have confidence in your ideas and you should express them and make your mark. You have the ability to have an impact, so make a statement, get involved in discussions, push your ideas forward especially when they are related to problem-solving in group situations. It's important to lead with ideas not only in work, but in your social life too.

This is a time when people are looking to you for advice and some guidance, so come out of the shadows and let your intelligence shine through.

You may be the person who has to cut through all the nonsense with some rational, reasonable thinking.

Affirmation: "I think clearly in dynamic situations and bring reason to group situations."

Love and Romance

Virgo could be compulsively drawn to someone you know it's not good for you, you almost want to go for people that you wouldn't have considered before because you know you need to discover something new about yourself, and that may mean pursuing people who are opposite or unsuitable.

Relationships that are the antithesis of what you've gone for in the past could be to the key to self-discovery. Sometimes you are subconsciously drawn to somebody (a friend or lover) that you don't really need in your life and yet you need to learn a lesson from that particular relationship.

This month you will tend to have revealing and emotionally complex interactions with other people, particularly in terms of love relationships. It's very important not to underestimate the feelings or motivations of your partner or new romantic partner as it is very important to be aware of games, manipulation and hidden agendas on the part of your partner, new romantic partner or business partner.

Not everything is what it seems right now, it's important to be observant, alert and to play your cards close to your chest. You are likely to feel very emotional during this period and relationships that don't contain enough depth can feel unsatisfying and unfulfilling.

Career and Aspiration

Virgo may suddenly question the path you're been on, even if it's been satisfying up to now, if your awakening has not happened yet, this is the month where you really begin to feel the impetus for a whole new ethos in your life.

You are captivated by a whole new life and career direction that promises adventure and more fulfilment, but this is not yet built on a workable foundation as the things that interest you tend to be brand new and slightly pioneering.

It's important for you to be flexible in your approach and ready to appreciate that the external forces, socially and economically, that aren't going back.

You must take the good with the bad with a positive attitude, loss and confusion are quite usual during this month and although it will be more difficult to build solid structures, it's certainly possible to generate inspirational ideas and plans.

So much of what's happening now seems to be out of your control, but you have the faith and sense of adventure to embrace these challenge and lead others through too.

It's very important now to have a bold and powerful message in terms of getting ahead in your career or with whatever goals you have set yourself. You must be by certain of what your intention is and then you must be effective in planning and moving head by communicating with others effectively.

Now all these are part and parcel of your nature, so should come easy to you, but just remember that right now people have short concentration spans and people are bombarded with information, so you've really got to work hard to ensure that your message cuts through. So you'll have to make it really accessible and understandable, so the key right now is a laser beam style of impactful communications to supercharge your career or impress your superiors.

Adventure and Motivation

June is a month when you may chase many different interests than usual, and you're up for experiences and adventures that take you out of your comfort zones.

Your curiosity is driving you crazy and you're after information and could suddenly take a long trip for no particular reason.

You enjoy the company of strangers. Your own eccentricities often are supercharged, but you're unapologetic and you tend to display more leadership and character, since you're likely to experiment rather than to remain tied to past paradigms.

Marriage and Family

Virgo tends to be pragmatic, but you're rarely controlling and the important lesson in June is to make you and your partner aware of how little control you guys actually have on any particular situation and that no matter how much you may want a certain result, you will often end up surprised with the final result or destination.

It's important for you and your partner to re-embrace faith and to be optimistic and mutually supportive as it all really comes down to believing that things will work together for good, and circumstances will tend to affirm that faith.

Praying or saying affirmations together can be incredibly powerful, so don't face the future with trepidation, affirm the positive and do it together.

This is a month when you tend to be more focused on personal goals, your own needs and the aspirations you have. Sometimes you may have a vague sense that your partner is holding you back, and that may cause a little bit of resentment, so it's very important for you to think about whether your partner is indeed holding you back and if there needs to be a discussion about that, or whether it possible just reflects your own anxiety which your projecting onto your partner.

Money and Finance

Managing cash flow is very important as while this is an excellent time for new beginnings, whatever you sets in motion tends to gain a life of its own and can get out of control burning through cash.

A degree of uncertainty is unavoidable so you have to take it a day at a time and monitor how it goes.

It's important for you to develop new relationships of trust with suppliers, distributors or experts who can help you in the new fields you're entering.

Luck tends to be on your side, however a lot depends on your outlook and the faith that you hold, because an optimistic outlook is more likely to attract favorable results now than usual.

Living and Loving to the Full

Variety is the spice of life.

This month you should embrace any time you encounter unexpected, sudden or even disconcerting experiences in love.

During this month change keeps the spark of love alive and thriving. Boredom should not be a problem.

Embracing spontaneity and inspiring the eccentricities within yourself and your partner can bring closer and could ignite positive vibes, even if they produce effects that you wouldn't expect.

Planetary Cautions

This month you have to avoid temptation, temptation of the flesh and the soul.

You must be aware of inflated promises, or getting in over your head. Suddenly changing or unusual circumstances make it difficult for you to distinguish between hype and the real deal.

Due to the fact that you're emotionally open and impressionable in June, you're more likely to get swept away with events with less discernment. You're often a long way down a road before you've seen things for what they are and then it can be hard to make a U turn without some conflict.

The problem right now is that there is no right or wrong that can be distinguished through reason or logic, you have to go with your gut, but your first instincts may be incorrect and so you must be prepared to backtrack at some point.

Essence and Energies – "In the stillness of remembering what you had"

This month is an excellent time to get in touch with the hidden sides of your own personality, it's important to understand your dreams and themes that reoccur so that you can get more clues about your unconscious and what is it that it's trying to tell you.

This can be a powerful month for meditation, going on retreats or engaging in activities which help you to reflect and gain understanding.

Sometimes you like to go off by yourself: this is certainly a time where independence is very important, you need to be a free spirit and you may want to take a long road trip or just roam-free taking long walks just to get away from it or and reconnect with your core.

Affirmation: "I chose to be free, I chose to be me."

Love and Romance

In your relationships, consistency is really important and so is having empathy. It may be time in a new relationship to start sharing secrets and developing trust, however trust is very fragile this month and it can easily be broken. Thus even if you have really intense conversations, they don't always go the way you planed, simply because you're beginning to discover your partner's more painful memories and triggers and that can bring up some emotions that may be difficult to deal with.

During this month, it's very important for Virgo and your partner to have a bit of privacy, it may not be advisable to be socializing with friends, going on double dates or hanging out in large groups. It's a better time to spend time with each other bonding and deepening the relationship, rather than simply cruising along being mainly distracted by friends, rather than working on your relationship.

Career and Aspiration

This month Mars enters Virgo, this signifies a time of great action and of you becoming more assertive, this is certainly a time to act now and get things done.

The motto this month is :talk is cheap', if you want something done, you better get on with it and do it yourself, there's no use beating around the bush or procrastinating, this is the time to dive right in.

It's important for you to show others that you mean business, that you have boundaries and you should stand up for yourself and not be pushed around.

This is an excellent time for leadership in practical matters and for repairing things, working on problems and reaching deadlines.

This is a less favorable time for intellectual pursuits, it favors jobs requiring physical muscle, self-motivation, drive and energy.

While it's important to be determined and action orientated this month, it's also important to be a free thinker, it's all about doing things where you feel a true connection to your own purpose, and sometimes before you really launch into a new project, a period of thoughtfulness, where you have time to work out your strategy clearly, is very important.

Adventure and Motivation

Because you have a high level of get up and go, you definitely need an outlet for this heightened energy level as you can be easily angered and can become irritable if you're doing very routine, repetitive and uninspiring work.

This is why it's best for you to get on with the hands on side of your business or work like getting more organized, motivating colleagues, getting rid of clutter or tackling technical problems, because sitting at a disc and grinding through paperwork can be incredibly boring for you.

If you are not getting much excitement or stimulation from your day job, it's very important for you to engage in competitive sports, outdoorsy activities or very physically demanding activities to release frustration and

58

any pent-up anger.

Marriage and Family

This is a good time for creative change in relationships: because you feel more vigorous and more assertive it can be a good time to tackle any problems within the household, the family or in your relationship.

This is a time when you need to get things off your chest, it is not a month to sweep things under the carpet or to put up and shut up, in some cases there could be a certain amount of friction as you redraws boundaries and re takes the initiative in relationships.

It's important for you to be alpha, to project power and show leadership in love even if your partner feels slightly threatened by your more assertive side, you can help both your partner and yourself to feel more in control and secure by showing a willingness to tackle internal and external problems head on. You must show you means business and act decisively.

It's important during this phase not to lose sight of who you really are. You may feel that you have to be acquiescing or obsequious in order to create calm in your personal relationships or in business, and it's very important for you not over compromise or compromise on your values.

You and your partner may argue or bicker a lot more about day-to-day issues or priorities during this phase.

This month should be used to improve communication skills and interpersonal relationship techniques.

You may be confused about the state of your love life, misunderstandings and a certain clash in terms of values and priorities is indicated. It's a time of jostling in relationships, you need to hold the line and work towards balance in give and take. Don't be too people pleasing, however don't be selfish either. This is a period to work on your relationships and improve understanding and cooperation.

Money and Finance

This month the ruler of your money house is in Leo and it then turns retrograde, this means it is a very good month for creative, theatrical and musical careers.

Virgo who are in any career that requires a lot of inspiration and creativity will do well because you're able to draw on your muse and produce excellent results.

If you're involved in the healing and medical fields, you can also be particularly successful right now as you have greater perceptive power and compassion, which you can use to more successfully help your clients.

This is an excellent month for Virgo to start understanding the underlying trends affecting your business or the economy, so you need to be aware of subtle changes that could become big news in the future.

Living and Loving to the Full

This month Virgo should take the lead in love and romance, you should be the first to suggest new activities, new places to go and new brainwaves on how to enhance your home.

It's a great time for you to organize surprises, or for you and your partner to do things that are spontaneous and which cause you both to feel more vibrant and alive.

Enhancing love this month means getting in touch with your inner child and your playful spirit, so you guys should not be held back by the viewpoints, expectations or the social mores of others, you should go with your heart and let your hair down and have fun.

Planetary Cautions

This month Mercury moves into Leo, it's a good time to keep your own counsel, the less said the better, so you should be careful of what you communicate to others.

This month you should be a good friend by keeping secrets, you should not engage in gossip or believe what you hear on the grapevine, it's important for you to be discreet.

While it's important for you to be honest, what you say this month in love and career could be held against you, so you doesn't want to blurt something out in haste, because this may motivate others to use that as a weapon against you.

It's a good time for being thoughtful and contemplative, rather than racing to any conclusions no matter what the pressure.

Moon Magic

The new moon phase extends from the 17th of July to the 30th of July. This waxing phase is the perfect fortnight for new initiatives, setting plans, establishing goals, starting anything prospective and being proactive. This is the action phase, details below:

The waxing phase is not a great time for going in retreats or delving into the occult. You should be wary of entering dangerous vicinities or neighborhoods. It's not a good time for charitable or voluntary work.

Mediation may be less helpful. You should be careful of new contracts with larger corporate entities or government departments.

Not a good time for double dating, new romance or social activities aimed at romance. Not a favorable time to work with children or young people. Sporting and other competitive events are less successful.

A good time together make a good impression or be persuasive. Excellent for using rational and reason. Favorable for exams, public speaking and communications related activities. Great for new weight loss or health improvement initiatives or physiotherapy.

Essence and Energies – "Just like a prayer"

There is a strong desire in you to pay back favors, you have a peculiar sense of divine justice and you are keen to make ethical and fair decisions as you feel like you are being judged and karma will not look kindly on you should you get it wrong. In August, you err on the side of caution and you often give more than you need to in any situation as you want to be sure your slate is clean.

Studies that are of a religious or philosophical persuasion can be very enlightening and you can find great reward in thinking about your purpose as a person, your destiny and how you can change the world in a positive way. You want to get away from the rat race and 'give back' during this August.

Affirmation: "I understand life is a cycle and I know that my actions have consequences."

Love and Romance

This month's Virgo may be more inclined to formalize a relationship in some way, now while you are not that keen for commitment this year, you are more eager to create stability in your life this month and so you will contemplate some form of commitment in a new relationship, even if it isn't engagement or a big step up.

Often you can get important advice from your date who has a slightly different perspective and who may be able to impart some guidance, especially on spiritual level which really makes a difference.

This month saying sorry and being accountable for your actions certainly helps relationships to run smoothly, it's possible that due to work pressure and your general irritability level you may not always treat your partner as well as you would hope to, but a genuine apology sincerely made goes a long way.

You may yield, compromise and accommodate the needs and wishes of others to your own detriment, now I guess that could be good news for your partner on the receiving end, but just like when you stretch a piece of elastic too far or blow a balloon up to bursting point, it will all go pop at some stage. You often don't recognize immediately how imbalanced or unfair your relationships with others have become, but you will, and that discovery can have a marked impact on you. You will begin to realize the psychological and even physical toll these demanding relationships (be it work or family) take and you will gather strength and begin to exert influence and reassert your power in these situations.

Career and Aspiration

This is not a particularly good time for Virgo to look for feedback as your colleagues and superiors can be quite critical, and an unusually high standard of work is required. So this is a time where you need to be quite exacting and precise.

You are quite impatient for results at the moment and work can be slow and frustrating, but you should not take shortcuts as you need to stick with it and persevere, because that will pay dividends.

For Virgo who enjoy leadership and responsibility, there should be plenty of that as more lands up on your shoulders. This is not a good time to jump into something totally new because you could land up with more on your plate than you expect.

This month you often feel pulled in two directions, you may feel in the middle of two powerful opposing forces. In some cases, you are put in this situation by people close to you, who want you to take sides. You are fair minded and can see both sides of a story, but you would rather offer support or guidance than get involved directly.

However, it may be that people you know are at odds or even at war legally or emotionally, and they are trying to drag you into their mess. You are very good at taking a step back and seeing things with logic, not emotion, and you may be key to meditating and thus bringing sense to a situation that has become out of control.

64

Adventure and Motivation

This is another great month for physical activity and for improving your fitness. Your energies are still high and if you show commitment and are methodical, you can be extremely productive and that may mean extra time to spend on sports and personal development rather than on the day job.

This is a time where you feel that you're up to the challenge and the more you conquer adversity, the more your personal growth comes on in leaps and bounds. So while there are difficulties, frustrations and obstacles this month, you will persevere and overcome them and this will lead to a huge increase in self-esteem and self-worth, which will certainly feed back into your relationships and career ambitions in the coming months, helping you to be even more successful.

Marriage and Family

This is a month where Virgo may have less freedom simply because of the demands of your relationship, so it's important that your plough energy into showing commitment and solidifying the relationship.

Again it is very important for you to be pragmatic and get things done anything that your partner has been nagging about or which you're neglected, as it will now become urgent and you have to face up to certain realities.

Thus this is definitely a month where it's nose to the grindstone, and where you and your partner must both show a commitment to relationship priorities and family needs.

It's not always the most light-hearted month, but it's certainly a month where you were both feel a sense of pride and achievement at the end of it, as long as you don't procrastinate and you bite the bullet.

Money and Finance

This month self-control is very important when it comes to money, you should delay making any outlays or spending on any significant considered purchase or new investing.

Often information available right now is inaccurate or incomplete and therefore you are not able to make a sensible decision, and even if you thinks that you have it all under control, there could be an unexpected twist in the tail.

With Mars in your first house, you can also be impulsive and can give in to whims and desires that lead you to spend money on momentary satisfaction, which in hindsight was a waste of resources.

Living and Loving to the Full

This is a great month for Virgo and your partner to turn over a new leaf, so if you guys had felt stale and uninspired, this is an excellent time to resolve to make changes and develop new attitudes.

It's not necessarily doing anything specific, it's about you and your partner developing a different mindset that can help take the relationship in a slightly different and exciting direction.

So it's time for you and your partner to examine anything that you s feel is holding you back from expressing your emotions, from having a better sex life or from improving the level of affection, and to talk about this honestly.

It's important to express how pressures from work, the children or both your parents are bringing you down and it's important that you are honest with each other, and can therefore use your relationship once again for the sanctuary it should be.

Planetary Cautions

Venus is retrograde in Leo right now, this means that certain activities that require an awful lot of self-confidence and self-esteem may not be ideal for you.

This isn't the best time for new relationships and it definitely isn't the best time for an affair, a fling or any relationship that has to be kept secret, although the possibility for this may arise.

You need to try as hard as you can to be straightforward in relationships because it's all too easy for game playing and emotional manipulation to become the order of the day, and you must watch out for signs that a partner is exaggerating or using emotion in a negative way to control you.

Mercury is retrograde until the 24th meaning you're quite erratic and you need time to think. You enjoy in depth conversations and study however you won't reach conclusions, you like to keep an open mind. You won't and shouldn't make any concrete decisions during this time, you need to fence sit and keep options open.

You will definitely make plans, analyses alternatives and start weighing up options, but it's much too soon to jump and commit to any new direction.

It's important not to play the blame game, it's easy to fall out with friends, associates or lovers over temporary disagreements or perhaps in some cases you feel that they are actively detracting from or thwarting your plans, but it's not as big as you think and certainly not worth ruining a friendship over. No set of people agree all the time, and differences of opinion and the odd bust up should be seen as creative and even informative, and so simmer down and let your friends etc. sit this one out if they cannot support you.

Moon Magic

The new moon phase extends from the 16th of August to the 30th of August. This waxing phase is the perfect fortnight for new initiatives, setting plans, establishing goals, starting anything prospective and being proactive. This is the action phase, details below:

This is an excellent time for positive visualization, affirmations and using positive thinking to supercharge your ambitions. It's a very important time for spiritual awareness, spiritual awakening and also personal development.

Dreams are particularly significant and maybe precognitive, your ESP is enhanced as is your intuition and you need to focus on spiritual awareness.

This is also a great time for retreats, goals involving groups and travelling with groups of people. Networking is successful.

This is a great period for your finances, cash flow improves. It's a positive months for investing, buying new assets and gaining new clients. A good month for financial analysis and changes.

This is a great time for teaching, academic studies and also publishing. Long distance travel and international business relations are favored, relations with the in-laws can be improved.

A good zone for property and home improvements, a positive period for entertaining with the family and hosting family events or having family to stay.

Another excellent time for health, fitness and medical matters. A good time to improve your health with alternative and holistic means. A great time to start new diet.

This is not a good period to get married or engaged however.

Venus is still retrograde Venus is still retrograde indicating an important time for resolving past issues dealing with personal emotional trauma and an important time to keep secrets and to maintain privacy in relationships.

Essence and Energies – "Saving the sweetest days"

The essence this month is patience, you may feel that many things are coming to a head and you are eager to see results, and in some cases you are eager for resolution or information, but the key right now is biding your time. There are certain things which will have to develop and come to light and there may be things happening behind the scenes that you are unaware of. So it's key to withstand some restlessness and some uncertainty, because there is a waiting phase that you are within right now and that is why is important for you to be patient.

This is an important time because the outcome of a lot of your projects or initiatives now will have more effect on your future than usual, and this is why it's so important to be patient to make sure that you have found the right solution to any problem areas.

It may be necessary to endure some limitations at the moment, but this will give you the necessarily time to think, get organized and get more prepared, both emotionally and philosophically.

Affirmation: "I am strong enough to ride through each hurdle with patience and tenacity."

Love and Romance

This can be an excellent month for love and romance and yet it can also be a difficult one for boundaries because although you are more compassionate, thoughtful and helpful, sometimes you can allow yourself to be depleted by any toxicity that your partner is harboring.

So while this month you get a great deal of satisfaction of out of showing your love in thoughtful and compassionate ways, you do have to remember to stay strong in your own mind and resist too much codependency in a new relationship.

Virgo need to be careful of new relationships that are starting with an imbalance, where your new partner is excessively needy and likely to become dependent on you very quickly. It can be very intoxicating having a partner who is extremely affectionate towards you, but could that be a sign of over compensation due to insecurity?

If there is a really good balance in the relationship and you guys are equally secure in yourselves, this can be a fantastic month for escapism, sexual experimentation and sharing each other's fantasies.

Career and Aspiration

In terms of career you need to keep doing what you're doing and play for the break, this is a time when you have to learn from your mistakes, but there's no need for you to become discouraged.

It's very important for you to not take the things that happen now personally, events good and bad are merely part of an organic process that you must work through. It's not that any particular person has it in for you or that you are essentially having any bad luck, you are simply needing to weather some storms, learn lessons and adjust in the way Virgo do, through observation and strategy.

Things are soon going to turn around for you and will move in a different direction, so you need to stay positive and get ready for the turnaround.

Because Mercury is retrograde in Virgo, in your first solar house this month, it's important to circle back to make sure that all the necessary elements of your plans are solid. This is the time when you are more likely to be criticized or put under the microscope and so you can preempt this by making sure that you are diligent and certain about your own objectives.

This is time when you need to make sure that everything that you're doing is working together towards your goal. So often we have a mission that we are focused on, but we end up engaging in self-defeating behavior, going on tangents or doing things that are not central to the thing we most want to achieve. So right now it's important for you to shut out distractions, for you to go over what your key objectives are, and then to make sure that everything that you are doing aligned neatly with those key objectives

Adventure and Motivation

This month it's important for Virgo to play an active role in your fate, you should not just stand and take what life is dishing up to you, and just hope for things to get better. This is a time to develop strategies and positive attitudes about improving your situation or speeding up the road back to recovery, particularly if you hasn't been well.

In the past months, because of the retrograde planets, there were some frustrations which may have caused a dent in your confidence, but you should not feel discouraged as adversity is a natural part of the unfolding of your personality and personal development this year. You must remember that at the start of this year you began things you're never done before, so you're on a learning curve and you are still on that learning curve, it's part of the adventure and you should embrace it.

Marriage and Family

In marriage, Virgo needs to stay on your toes, this is not a time for taking your partner or the marriage for granted. You need to keep working on showing loyalty and showing commitment, just because you're in a stable relationship or marriage doesn't mean your partner necessarily feels secure, so you must do things and reinforce the perception that this is indeed a committed loving relationship.

The message this month is that you can't just rest on your laurels, even if the relationship is going fairly well, this month there needs to be a renewed effort at showing your partner that you cares, being a tender and considerate, doing simple things like phoning if you're going to be late, taking your fair share of the responsibility and being thoughtful.

This is certainly a revealing time relationships, where you understand the value of give and take and the extent of give and take that is acceptable to you.

Everything in life is about contrast, and the bad times provide the contrast and the perspective that you need to recognize the beauty and the uniqueness of your relationship. So what's important this month, is not only to appreciate your partner, but to appreciate the journey that you are on with your partner, and to understand that the journey is an important part of the unfoldment of your life, and is a totally unique and therefore beautiful experience.

Money and Finance

With Mars going into Libra, this is an excellent month for improving your take-home pay packet. It's a great time to start a side hustle or to use your skills and talents to start a new income stream - if you're on a set salary. If you're on commission there is a direct relationship between hard work and sales, so working extra hard could mean you obtain wonderful targets and have a bumper month in terms of income.

It may be necessary for you to work a lot harder at getting new clients and customers, so there may need to be renewed effort in marketing, promoting or good communication with clients and customers to upsell or stimulate demand for your products.

It's no good waiting for things to pick up, you need to be proactive and do what you can to keep things moving in the right direction.

Living and Loving to the Full

This September key to enhancing love magic is that you must accept that they are always ups and downs is love and life, you need to appreciate the texture of loving! If one only experiences the smooth one would become less appreciative of what one has, it's the rough that makes the smooth feel that much more beautiful.

Everything in life is about contrast, and the bad times provide the contrast and the perspective that you need to recognize the beauty and the uniqueness of your relationship. So what's important this month, is not only to appreciate your partner, but to appreciate the journey that you are on with your partner, and to understand that the journey is an important part of the unfoldment of your life, and is a totally unique and therefore beautiful experience.

Planetary Cautions

Mercury goes direct on the 16th of September, but before that time is not ideal for the negotiations, short journeys or public speaking.

Virgo need to be well aware of nuance and also deception because nothing is as it seems.

You are more likely to have to deal with tricky and duplicitous people or it may be that you are dealing with unreliable people who have no bad intentions, but the bottom line is that you can't necessarily rely on what other people say or the information they give you. You need to be cautious in all your dealings, particularly financial, with other people.

This is not a good time to schedule any educational or speaking events, because things are bound to go awry and you may hit the wrong notes with your audience.

Moon Magic

The new moon phase extends from the 14th of September to the 29th of September. This waxing phase is the perfect fortnight for new initiatives, setting plans, establishing goals, starting anything prospective and being proactive. This is the action phase, details below:

This time the waxing period is tricky for any group or social goals, particularly to do with politics, humanitarian and charitable issues.

This phase pragmatic matters are more important than spiritual and personal development goals.

This is an excellent period for buying property, renovating or home improvements, it also favors family events. This is an excellent time for new business to do with hospitality and catering or literature.

This is a good zone for financial affairs, for new investment, improving cash flow and buying assets for your business. This is also a good time for improved reputation via word-of-mouth. This period favors publishing, advertising and long-distance travel for business or pleasure.

Essence and Energies – "Dust out the demons inside"

The essence this month is saying YES.

While communication, information and career are strong themes this month, you must act with solid intention. This month you can really knuckle down and make solid progress on life goals and ambitions; suddenly the plans are clear and no longer vague. It is like you got the go ahead. It could be that you have been in a planning phase up until now: applying for loans or grants, getting business plans together, looking for premises, finding the right university, looking for a job and now this month you get the YES, you were after and suddenly the planning is over and you have to go and do it for real. This can also mark the end of a trail or probation period where you were supervised to see if you could handle the role and it can also mean the end of an apprenticeship or training period – you are now fully fledged and ready to get stuck in.

Affirmation: "I have earned my stripes, I have done the hard work and I'm ready to shine.

Love and Romance

This is a very important time for you to meditate and listen to your inner voice for guidance. There may be some indecision or some doubts about the way your new romance is developing and your inner voice can guide you to the right outcome as long as you are patient.

The big problem with Virgo this year is impatience, high expectations and jumping to conclusions, and that it what's probably causing some problems in a current love relationship. Which is why being patient, being cool and not trying to preempt things or rush things along is very important to this month.

New relationships start fast, as attraction is like striking a match this month, your chart is all about action, so not much thought goes into it which can mean obvious problems get overlooked and your partner may wind up saying later on, "You never told me," and you will say, "But you never asked.". The main question is really, "why does it matter?" and can either of you answer that.

It's time in love relationships for you to get a more balanced spiritual perspective and to get into a good mindset for making the right choices going forward. It's no good trying to make decisions when you are in a frenzied and rather aggravated state.

Career and Aspiration

During this month Virgo can benefit from organic growth and repeat custom, however you're almost waiting for something to happen, waiting for the next shoe to drop, you may feel a bit anxious as you feel something big is around the corner. It may be that you are waiting for the approval of a new project/proposal, the result of a job application or an important client to get back to you. It can be a nail biting time and it's important for you to use your positive affirmations and to envisage the best outcome in your mind.

So there's a slight feeling of being on hold or treading water, however you shouldn't neglect to acknowledge all the great things that are happening by putting too much focus on one particular exciting element of your work. You have to see your work in the totality and you may just have to switch yourself away from a fixation on one particular client or one particular aspect of your work, because you could be losing site of other important clients and customers.

Adventure and Motivation

This month it's really important for you to let go and that can mean letting go of material things and past attachments. This is an excellent month for a total clear out, for going minimalist, for simplifying your office and generally getting rid of anything you no longer uses.

It's important to free up space in your home, your office or any place where there's clutter developing, as this can be creating energy blockages. Right now you're waiting for something to happen and for a new energy to come into your life, but maybe there's something you need to let go of first for this adventure thing to enter.

Marriage and Family

This month there can be arguments and bickering in marriage, particularly about money issues and priorities. There may be periods of tension between Virgo and your children and you must refrain from being too critical or putting too much pressure up on them.

You can be quite possessive in love and your pride is easily hurt by rejection or lack of loyalty, your standards for your partner are high, maybe even unreasonable and that can be quite restricting for them. You are protective over your partner and want to do things to win them over, your energy when it comes to romance is high and you are quite romantic. Your passions are strongly stirred and your sex drive is high, in all relationships you will seek to improve the physical side and yet you may not be tender or patient.

Often problems in the marriage are due to Virgo and your partner not putting sufficient boundaries between then and the children. It's important as parents for you both to take authority and not to try to be the children's best friends otherwise you lose their respect.

During this month it is important for Virgo and your partner to redefine or reframe the relationship you have with your children, or your respective children if there are step children involved, and this should involve better communication, clear boundaries and restoration of respect for the older generation. It's time for parents to act like parents.

Money and Finance

This month the competition is intense and it's very important for Virgo to focus on detail and perfection. In any cut-throat, competitive industry where there is a lot at stake, it can be even more ruthless and intense than usual and so you need to be at your most ingenious.

Getting it right and following through counts, therefore if you're to earn top dollar, you have to stay with it right until the end. This is not a time for a quick wrapping up of any projects, you have to go out with a bang.

This may be a fairly climactic time when certain projects reach a head, or crucial phase and that can be quite nerve-racking.

In some instances you need to know when to quit while on top, this could particularly pertain to the stock market, you need to get out before you get burnt.

Living and Loving to the Full

This could be an exciting time in Virgo 's fantasy life, often we feel stuck or restricted and we are not really in touch with what we are feeling, but this year Virgo has had a sudden change in focus and this may have changed the way you feel about yourself. Therefore it's time to widen your boundaries and change the parameters of your emotional and love life, and to embrace either conversations about sexual matters or other conversations which you never would have before.

In terms of sex life, it can also be fun playing with identities and you guys may want to dress up, use props or do roleplay, simply to explore different sides of your nature and also open up channels of communication and understanding.

Often roleplay allows you to say things to each other that you wouldn't say if you were being yourselves.

Planetary Cautions

Balance and moderation are very important in health, you may not be eating or sleeping well right now and you're probably not getting enough exercise. This is a time when you're probably doing too much snacking and going to the coping foods like coke, wine and ready meals.

Your sleep pattern is quite a disrupted and you need to try and get into a calmer state with meditation for relaxation and by avoiding the sorts of foods which are likely to overstimulate you before bed.

It's not yet time for a detox or a new diet, it's simply time for balance, moderation and incorporating more fresh food and fresh air into your lifestyle, and staying away from the devices for a certain amount of hours a day.

Moon Magic

The new moon phase extends from the 14th of October to the 28th of October. This waxing phase is the perfect fortnight for new initiatives, setting plans, establishing goals, starting anything prospective and being proactive. This is the action phase, details below:

This is an excellent time for positive visualization, affirmations and using positive

This can be quite intense waxing phase, it's very emotional and dream interpretation or past life regression can be particularly useful as you analyses underlying psychological factors.
This is not a good time for getting involved in politics, protests or large group movements and activism.

This is a tricky period for brand new romance, internet dating or social activities aimed at meeting other people. This is not an ideal time for decisions to do with children or businesses involving new technology and invention.

Essence and Energies – "Stirring to action"

The essence to embrace this month is novelty and excitement.

You must do things and go places that you have never tried or been before and life will suddenly feel freer, which is perfect for the curious Virgo nature and can herald a feeling of renewal.

You should not accept rules or restrictions and those who try and tie you down risk arousing the tiger in you as you have that quick witted ability to deliver a stinging retort on display. This is not however a selfish energy, as you have the potential to change others as well, you wish to liberate people in your life and convince them to hop on board and join your band of brothers - you can be somewhat of a ring leader, stirring others to action, but be careful what you start as it may get out of control.

Affirmation: "Nothing can restrict me only my own integrity."

Love and Romance

Sometimes this month, you can say words in haste which end up damaging understanding. You are still in a rather impatient mood, there's a lot on your mind and often when Virgo has a lot playing on your mind, you can become critical, quite tense and a little bit abrupt.

A partner may perceive you as quite cold, aloof or detached, so you need to communicate successfully with your partner about anything from work that may be bothering you, or any problems that are weighing on your mind. You need to make a partner understand that part of your energy is taken up this month by work problem-solving, and quite a high stress level as well as demanding schedule, and therefore you're not being cold or aloof, it's just that you're got a lot on your plate.

They say that 'a stitch in time saves nine', and some kind words and time spent explaining to a partner why you're not as available as usual go a long way to keep the relationship on track.

Relationships are intense and complicated this month. You can experience an unconscious and compulsive attraction to another that baffles yet excites you. In current relationships you will experience strong reactions and can be turned on and off quickly. Things that annoy you about your partner will be even more annoying than usual and the things you like will make your melt. You can go from 0-100 in a few moment when it comes to feeling sexual and also in terms of getting angry, but you are full of passion.

Relationships can open you up and teach you more about yourself this month; in fact relationships are a forum for transformation and the confrontation of issues that dog you.

Career and Aspiration

This month you need to be both cautious and observant, while many times this year the overarching picture was important, this month the detail is crucial, and you have to make sure you pays attention to the small things that can ultimately lead to success or failure.

There can be some considerable changes to the communication and information technology sphere which will impact the way you do business.

It may be necessary that you takes a business trip to sort out a problem. This is certainly a month where problems tend to be tricky to deal with, and sometimes what's on the surface belies a greater problem on a deeper level that needs to be understood and worked out.

So you shouldn't think any problem this month will be solved quickly, although you can still solve it with sustained effort.

Adventure and Motivation

This month it's all about being willing to close the door and open the window, you should be ready for change and ready to bring about endings in order to facilitate new beginnings.

This month a sudden opportunity may arise that can be quite transformational, but it will involve you moving out of some mental comfort zones. So often events this month are exciting, but at the same time they challenge your preconceived ideas, beliefs and perceptions. Thus often there's a hard pill to swallow in that you may have to accept that you was wrong about something in the past, however the more willing you are to acknowledge a mistake or an incorrect altitude, the more you can take advantage and move ahead quite quickly on a new opportunity.

Marriage and Family

This is a month when you and your partner may shop around for things to improve the home, you s may be thinking ahead to planning family events or gatherings for Thanksgiving or the festive season, and maybe a time when you and your partner have more reason to discuss decorating, furnishing and catering arrangements in the home.

It's certainly a good time to welcome friends and neighbors into your home, and this can help you both to feel more comfortable and relaxed. So sometimes entertaining others can be a key way to bring about more cooperation and healing in the relationship.

If you and your partner are in business together this can also be an excellent time for entertaining colleagues or even the boss, or possibly having an event for your prospective clients together. This is a month where Virgo s who are in business together with their partners can work very successfully to create prosperity.

Money and Finance

This is a good month for Virgo s who make money in the fields of law, negotiation and the beauty industry.

Key to making money this year is being diplomatic, paying attention to customer service and image. It's very important that your office or front of shop is appealing and comfortable as looks and presentation count. You have to make sure that your customers have the best experience whether they visit you in person or on the website.

It's probably time to pay attention to aesthetics and finishing touches, so things like fresh flowers in your work place, consulting room or your office and magazines scattered around, ambient music or fragrance etc. little things like that that make new clients particularly feel more welcome and is thus very helpful.

This is a good month for money. If you believe in the power of attraction is it a great time to use that technique to draw resources towards you. It is not just about money, it is also about having access to facilities or clubs or a company car that will enhance your life or ability to do your job.

A great deal of physical energy and positivity mean you can take on more than you can handle and still win, you have courage and the courage of conviction, and goals usually have a monetary and a spiritual element which means you feel it in your bones and your timing is right. While new goals can have quite substantial initial outgoings and sunk cost in terms of material input and effort, there will encouraging signs from early on.

Living and Loving to the Full

Relationships with brand new people you have never met before are quite magical. Positive new relationships are likely to be connected to new starts you are making. Physical attraction plays a large role in new love as does adventure and taboo breaking. New relationships are exciting but quite nerve wracking as they threaten to disrupt both your status quo and your perceptions of life.

So you should get ready for a love affair that will rewrite your rules and your script for your life, as your priorities could be ready for an earthquake.

Love life tends to be fuel injected and you may feel the thrust like when a plane takes off as you meets a potential new beau. The relationship may not head for full blown dating right away, there may be a period of cat and mouse as you s feel each other out and play somewhat of teasing, flirting game.

Planetary Cautions

This may not be the best time for home renovations and major changes to the home. Any big property deal or home improvement undertaken now could contain hidden pitfalls or may take a lot longer than expected.

This month family matters need patience and some focus, so the key words when it comes to marriage and anything surrounding the home are tolerance and perseverance.

Sometimes this month things can seem on top of you and you can make mountains out of molehills, the important thing to remember is things are not as bad as they seem, there is simply a lot to deal with during this month and you're slightly tired and a little bit mentally drained, and that can cause a pessimistic attitude.

Moon Magic

The new moon phase extends from the 13th of November to the 27th of November. This waxing phase is the perfect fortnight for new initiatives, setting plans, establishing goals, starting anything prospective and being proactive. This is the action phase, details below:

This waxing phase again is not ideal for spiritual and philosophical goals, it's not great for meditation, retreats or secret love affairs and flings. You should be cautious about meeting new friends or pursuing new romantic or networking goals.

This is not ideal for social, humanitarian or political goals, also not favorable for attending very large events.

It is also a good time for career development, new business directions, dealing with authority, PR and public speaking. Dealing with animals is not favored, this is not a good month for a radical new diet. Recruiting staff or outsourcing is not favored.

DECEMBER

Essence and Energies – "I can see clearly now the rain has gone."

Perception and insight are the key essences this month. Resolution before the New Year is important.

Your powers of perception are sharp and this is a good time to make wise decisions which encompass long and short term goals and which take account of the impact on people. Your judgement can be relied upon to be excellent and you are fair and decisive. Your ability to be in touch with and incorporate group opinions will make your decisions and the way you go about your job broadly acceptable, if not welcomed.

Use your essential ability to rationalize to resolve differences you have had with family members, suppliers or issues in your recent past, in an amicable and mutually beneficial way: you are able to be persuasive and forceful enough to ensure differences are smoothed over and put to bed. This will help end the year on a high with no lingering problems to deal with next year.

Affirmation: "I see clearly to the heart of the matter, my mind is unbiased and I seek fairness and resolution."

Love and Romance

While December is a good month for love apart from what I have said about the retrograde period, sometimes Virgo are inclined to be a touch insincere and you may use a diplomacy as a way of avoiding certain issues. You are certainly keen to side step things and do not want to have difficult conversations this month.

You are keen on having fun, larking around, making jokes and enjoying yourself, and you may not be very patient with a partner who is seeking more attention or compassion.

This is a good month if your partner can hold his own and is not in a particularly needy state of mind, the more independent your partner is and willing to have fun and let his hair down the better. However, like I say if a partner wants to cling to you and becomes quite possessive, you can become incredibly invasive and insincere.

Career and Aspiration

This can be a time of intense effort and work behind the scenes. This is an excellent period for you to get organized, both in terms of research, technicalities and also with regards to any physical structures, assets or logistics that need to be arranged.

This can be an excellent time for Virgo who run their own businesses, and you may be incredibly busy fulfilling orders and dealing with new clients. Self-employed Virgo are often rushed off their feet.

This tends to be a very busy month for those Virgos in hospitality, catering and the care field, and yet you can find the work quite invigorating because it is stimulating and it involves quite a lot of movement which helps you not to become bored.

In terms of work, the year is going out with a bang so it's all hands on deck.

This is your opportunity to extend you potential or improve your business by using your ability to create a very personal connection with people, which can give you the edge in either providing for them, giving them better service or helping them. You are an excellent judge of character, which means that you can sense the weaknesses of others and use that to your advantage – you should not do this is a negative, selfish way, but rather in a way whereby working with that person you are both better off. Your work may bring you into contact with environmental issues, other people's family or real estate deals.

Adventure and Motivation

A lot of the Adventure and Motivation right now is all to do with planning for next year, so this is an excellent time for you planning holidays, long haul trips or special activities that you want to devote time to next year.

This is a particularly good time to contemplate a trip of a lifetime.

This is also an exciting time for you to reflect on everything you're achieved this year, the barriers you broke down, the limits and comfort zones that you escaped and spend time congratulating yourself and feeling proud of yourself.

They say that pride is one of the seven deadly sins, but
Virgos don't feel proud of themselves often enough so it's something you really should do this month.

Marriage and Family

This is a great month for you to get fully involved in family matters, events and parties. It's time to roll up your sleeves and show your enthusiasm. It may be important for you to bite your tongue and keep your temper in check when it comes to certain family members or possibly the in-laws. You don't quite appreciate interference and you can be rather short tempered, and any disagreements that you are likely to have with your partner this month, stem from the fact that your behavior with certain family members can leave something to be desired.

It may be that relationships have become rather controlling or restrictive recently. A deep discussion may have been put off as you are both too busy, too rushed or there are more pressing priorities. That good talk is way overdue: you need to set an evening aside to talk to your partner about where you are at in the relationship: what needs to change; how can you recapture romance; how can you adjust to each other's needs in a way which is fairer and how will you get more quality time together.

Money and Finance

This is an excellent month for money-making through a variety of activities, and so the more you can be versatile and multitask the better. Your income is enhanced when you pay attention to business communication and attention to detail in terms of staying in touch with clients and customers, and insuring everyone feels rewarded in some way, either through thanks or discounts.

While public relations is important, it's also vital that you touches base with all your important contacts, colleagues suppliers and members of your network to ensure that the relationships remain strong going into the next year and no one feels neglected.

Living and Loving to the Full

This month the way Virgo can improve your love life is through written communication, so writing old fashioned love letters, leaving little notes in surprising places that can be found by your partner unexpectedly etc. is excellent. This all shows tenderness, thoughtfulness and concern and can be a delightful new tool to show your partner you're thinking of them.

Of course it's the month where people exchange Christmas cards and yet these days it's less popular because of the expense, because of WhatsApp and messenger, but a good old fashioned Christmas card where you have made an effort to write more than TO and FROM, and has taken the time and trouble to put some special words in, can go a long way to enhancing romance and is an excellent way to go.

Written communication especially in your own handwriting is extremely personalized and thoughtful, and it's something that's overlooked in this day and age, but certainly enhances love.

Planetary Cautions

This month Mercury goes retrograde in Capricorn after the 13th of the month, therefore after the 13th is not a good time for dating, double dates for using dating apps, because matters to do with new romance and love become rather complicated and it creates a lot of miscommunication.

You should also be more careful with your electronic conversations and all social media posts in general because you don't want to convey the wrong message or say something in the heat of the moment that you later regrets.

When it comes to love, it's best for you to say what you want to say in person, so that you can gauge the reaction and can avoid the kind of misconceptions that often happen when one communicates - especially in haste – electronically.

Moon Magic

The new moon phase extends from the 12th of December to the 26th of December. This waxing phase is the perfect fortnight for new initiatives, setting plans, establishing goals, starting anything prospective and being proactive. This is the action phase, details below:

This waxing phase again is not ideal for spiritual or group activities. Networking, political activities and joining new organizations is not generally advisable.

Mercury retrograde in Capricorn from the 13th indicates that from then new romance, internet dating, long distance love and novel social activities are not successful.

The retrograde phase is also not ideal for brand new creative or artistic projects. Competitive activities and innovation are not successful.

Property matters, home improvements and entertaining family in your home is successful. A good time for businesses involving tourism, catering, hospitality and real estate.

Investing and money goals are lucky. A good time for purchasing stock or new assets.

Long term relationships get a boost.

Excellent for long haul travel and international holidays. A positive time for advertising, publicity and marketing.

Wrapping Up

Well that's a wrap of my biggest most comprehensive Virgo Horoscope yet.

Whether you are a Virgo or know a Virgo, I do believe you will have found this very helpful and informative.

I aim to give you a variety of advice based on psychology, spiritual insight, relationship advice and business guidance, so you get a little bit of everything.

Take care and have a wonderful 2023.

Blessings, Lisa.

Lightning Source UK Ltd.
Milton Keynes UK
UKHW011005291222
414562UK00001B/141